S o you know how mo ~~stuff~~ is about figuring out what is not working in your brain and teaching you coping skills and other such new tricks to make it work? And how they tell you that even if you feel like the rest of the world is crazy, the real answer lies within your own mental processes, self-control, and agency?

Well what if that weren't true? What if your brain is doing exactly what a healthy brain is designed to do... just in response to a threat? What if the trauma you have experienced, coupled with the power dynamics in the world around you are the problem, not you?

This is actually a *really* new idea in mental health. That's why adding Post Traumatic Stress Disorder to the DSM in 1980 was a huge undertaking—it meant recognizing that mental health diagnoses could have an external etiology. Which is just a fancy way of saying that humans can be broken by what happens to us, we aren't just fucked up because of whatever gene combination we inherit.

Flash forward a few decades. As we learn more about how the brain and body work and we learn more about how trauma (both individual and systemic) impacts the brain and body in the long term, we are realizing that many, if not most, mental health issues have either an external etiology or at least are greatly impacted by the world around us.

Maybe we didn't buy the ticket but it is now, officially, both our circus and our monkey.

Here's a framework that was developed by a bunch of smart people[1] for figuring out *why* your brain is freaking out at you.

---

1 Other mental health theories like Relational Cultural Theory, Liberation Theory, and Critical Race Theory have been advocating for a similar framework for decades. On the physical health side, physicians like Gary Kaplan (the Ultramind Solution guy) have been advocates for looking for processes instead of causes when providing treatment for some time, as well.

It's called the Power Threat Meaning (PTM) framework which is a fancy way of saying that specific power dynamics that you've felt threatened by at some point in (or throughout) your young development or adult life have caused your brain to create systems of meaning that produce the symptoms that have led to whatever your diagnosis. And if we considered the context of your life, we'd probably give and treat that diagnosis a lot differently.

Instead of saying that we are biologically wired for mental health and that negative events help bring those predispositions into being, here I am going to tell you about a theory that says it's the opposite. With very few exceptions, we aren't born with "broken brains," but our experiences (and the experiences of our biological family members, even!) create survival-based adaptations that cause mental health issues in the long term. We learn to survive through our engagement with the negative experiences imposed on us by people with power over us, whether it's an individual, a group, a culture, or a political system .

It's the trauma.

It's how culture impacts our day to day lives.

It's the toxic hierarchical structure of contemporary society that privileges certain experiences over others.

This is what creates what we call sickness.

Treating all mental health diagnosis as a broken brain isn't helpful. It does a huge disservice to all the surrounding life events that have impacted and/or contributed to that diagnosis. Everything that happens to us happens within the context in our lives. Understanding the role traumatic events have played in someone's clinical depression is just as important as understanding how someone's work in a coal mine contributed to their lung cancer.

When a mental health professional gives you a diagnosis, what they're typically doing is looking at your symptoms and seeing if they can find a label that matches what they see and/or what you tell them. With the exception of some neurological diagnoses (like autism spectrum disorders, intellectual disabilities, some forms of dementia, and some kinds of thought disorders) most of our diagnoses are based on this sort of guesswork. Basically, we look at what we can see behaviourally or what you tell us about your internal experiences and go down a checklist. For example, if you're listless, have bad hygiene, and have no interest in stuff? According to our checklist, you're suffering from clinical depression.

Ok, though. How might treatment be different if we approached this "depression" with the additional information regarding power, threat, meaning, and threat responses? It could be life changing and world changing, right? Not only would it provide more insight into how to help each individual person, it also begs for more social justice involvement. Staying well in a broken system is an almost impossible task. Unfortunately, systems change doesn't take place until it takes hold in the center...even if the margins had to shove it into that position inch by inch.

The PTM Framework, however, has the capacity to make these needed changes. Firstly because it came from a mainstream organization instead of a rowdy band of rabble rousers on the margins of the field. This means the decades of rabblerousing by queer folks, POC, and other marginalized individuals has infiltrated from the margins to the center and larger, cultural change is happening.

And secondly, the PTM framework is *good*. And thoughtful. And expansive. And inclusive. And generally a great structure from which to reconceptualize therapeutic and community care.

This model doesn't replace other practices or models of treatment. Most existing treatments are very helpful to recovery...*in their proper place.* And that proper place is understanding symptoms for what they are: Not signs of an underlying disease but as very human threat responses.

In psychology speak, this means adding a "contextual focus" in psychiatric diagnoses. So for instance, anxiety or depression or a personality disorder or bipolar doesn't occur because something's inherently wrong with you. It's given to you by your environment.

So how does the PTM framework work? It starts by asking the following questions:

[special format - these next four paras should have reverse indentation or some similar way to distinguish them as a list]

How has <u>power</u> operated in your life? What kinds of things happened to you because power was wielded over you in harmful ways? This could be anything from growing up with a domineering parent to experiencing systemic racism to living through a war.

What kinds of <u>threats</u> did this pose to you? How did this harmful use of power against you cause harm to you or otherwise affect you? For instance, maybe now you can't stand being around someone yelling, or maybe you lost a leg.

What <u>meaning</u> did you develop based on these situations and experiences to you? How did you make sense of these experiences? What did they tell you about the world and other people in it? Maybe you learned that all people in authority are potential threats to your safety, or that loud bangs mean you or someone around you will be hurt or killed.

What kind of <u>threat response</u> did you develop due to these events? What did you do to survive? How did you cope? How did you behave to protect yourself? So now you literally don't hear someone's words when they're yelling, or you feel compelled to physically attack any sort of authority figure.

[end special format]

So how do we infuse the PTM into healing work in a practical way? At the time of this writing, the framework hasn't been operationalized into practice anywhere.

But the PTM Framework authors have suggestions. One is that *narrative approaches* are an excellent tool. Meaning-making through storytelling is an inherent part of being human, and a way of being well in the world that long predates "therapy." The goal is to create a narrative of your experience in a way that includes your status as a survivor with the capacity to continue to grow and thrive.

So that is what this little workbook is. A place to unpack the narrative of your experience as a response to your experiences and a place to look at your capacity for growth and healing.

Unpacking Then

What events in your life had a negative impact on you? In other words, what scared you, threatened your security, harmed you or traumatized you? It's generally easier to compile this as a timeline in 5 year increments because it can be hard to remember things in great detail, especially from periods where we were really young and/or there was a lot going on.

Ages 0-5

Ages 5-10

Age 10-15

Age 15-20

Age 20-25

Age 25+

In addition, sometimes terrible things are normalized around us to the point that we don't even register them as traumatic...see the appendix at the end of this workbook for a list of possible traumatic events to see if there is anything you might have forgotten or missed. Go ahead and add them to your timeline and make a note here of what you realized merited adding.

What events had an impact on your parents and other caregivers?

How did those events inform their interactions with you?

What social systems were in place that exacerbated these negative experiences?

What social systems are in place that continue to operate as a barrier to healing in the present?

What were the consequences of your negative life events?

How did these events impact your daily life? Surroundings?

How did they impact your relationships at that time?

How did they impact your physical body?

How did they impact your view of yourself? What feelings did you notice? What did you tell yourself about your experience?

How did they impact your behaviors? Meaning...what did you need to do to survive?

What rules did you figure out about how the world works based on these events?

How did you come to define "normal" based on these experiences?

What labels were used to describe you (diagnoses, things people called you based on your behavior)?

Which of these labels are still used to describe you, either by others or by your internal voice?

How did you expect others to treat you and/or interact with you? We don't exist in isolation, but in interactions with others which we then use to create rules about the world. These rules are often in the form of "If I _____, other people will _____." Write down the rules you've learned:

If I am hurt, other people will:

If I am scared, other people will:

If I am angry, other people will:

If I am peaceful, other people will:

If I am honest, other people will:

If I am expressive, other people will:

If I am...

Unpacking Now

How does this all fit together to inform your present reality? What is your story of survival?

What skills did you develop to survive? Both in your external works and your internal understanding of these events?

What labels or descriptions best describe your experience?

What social and political systems are in place that limit your access to healing and wellness?

What makes you strong?

How do you demonstrate your strength?

What areas do you want to build strength in?

What would your life look like if things were ideal for you?

What systems changes would support that process?

What work do you need to do for your own self growth?

What assistance do you need from others that is in their power to provide?

What resources do you need to access?

Conclusion

Ideally, your answers to these questions can become an amazing tool for you to share with your therapist while you do work on figuring out healthier coping skills and newer neural pathways. I also know that may not be something you have access to for a multitude of reasons, and you may be doing this on your own for the time being.

Either way, this is an incredibly useful starting point. I often talk about how understanding our history and the patterns they have created is like putting something under the microscope for the first time. Not just because we are getting a closer look, but because in order to see what we are looking at we have to flip on a light. And the minute we do, whatever we are looking at will react to that light. Noticing is the biggest part of changing. And we can't negotiate with our body and brain if we don't know where the response is coming from, right? Building new patterns has to make sense...or we are going to revert back to the responses that made sense in the past.

So here's to the future.

List of potential traumas

Where does all that trauma come from? Here is a more inclusive, but still incomplete, list of common sources of trauma:

Child Abuse (physical, sexual, emotional, neglect): Child abuse is a huge category, and even the federal government has struggled to define it well. But essentially, any act (or failure to act/intervene) that harms a child or puts a child at imminent risk of harm is abuse. The younger the child, the more powerless and fragile they are, the more limitations there are to them being able to defend themselves or outcry, the more risk there is for serious, ongoing abuse.

Domestic/Intimate Partner Violence (physical, sexual, emotional, economic, psychological): Domestic violence is the adult version of child abuse, for lack of a better comparison. It occurs in intimate partner/romantic relationships among both youth and adults. You do not have to be sharing a living space with your romantic partner for it to be considered domestic violence.

The US Department of Justice notes a few differences in the types of violence that can occur in intimate partner relationships: Emotional abuse includes attacks on the partner's self-worth (e.g., criticism, name-calling). Psychological abuse is more action-oriented, and can consist of isolating the partner, threatening harm to them or others that they care about, or destroying items that have meaning to them (without physically abusing them or other people). Economic abuse focuses on the way a partner creates a situation wherein they have all economic control in the relationship, forcing the abused partner to remain with them (controlling all money, or not letting them have a job or get job training, for example).

Elderly/Disabled Adult Abuse (physical, sexual, emotional, neglect, exploitation): Unlike the above category, where the relationship is considered an equal one (until manipulated to be otherwise), some adults are considered by law to be powerless and fragile, and therefore have the same protections under the law that children are due. These individuals include older adults and individuals with physical or mental health impairments. The one main difference between child abuse and elderly/disabled abuse is the concept of exploitation. An adult with income (for example, social security or retirement income) may have the use of that income exploited by another individual. While many adults have individuals who help them manage their money effectively, making sure their needs are met, there are many others who go without basics because that money is being mismanaged by their "caretaker."

Impaired Caregiver: Unlike in the above cases, caregivers who are not causing intentional harm or neglectful practices may still have their own impairments that make it difficult to render care, which can have a negative impact on the individuals they care for. For example, a child with a parent being treated for cancer may struggle with not having all their needs met due to the illness of the caretaker coupled with the anxiety of seeing the illness and decline of the person who is their primary means of support and one of the people they love most in the world.

School Violence: School violence can consist of one-time, sentinel events (like a school shooting), or be the product of chronically dangerous school conditions (gang warfare, drug use, drug sales, fighting, etc.). If an individual is engaged in a school environment, and witnesses, partakes in, or is a victim of violence within it, that can be considered a traumatic event.

Community Violence: Living or working in certain communities can also pose a risk for trauma exposure. We can experience one time, sentinel events (again, such as a shooting), or be exposed to violence on a regular basis by the nature of the common experiences found in the community to which we are exposed (drug use, fighting, etc.). Most community violence can be tied to neighborhoods that have been left impoverished of hope, opportunity, and money. Many of the other categories could also fall under the broad category of "community violence," but are widespread enough to merit their own section.

Bullying/Cyberbullying: Bullying is the use of one's strength or influence to control the actions of another. It can include real violence, the threat of violence, or intimidation to wield power over another. The traditional form of bullying is the older kid taking the lunch money of the younger one. But in the digital age, bullying can take many different forms. Electronic communication allows new ways of bullying to take place—from a distance and with anonymity in an increasing number of cases. This has allowed individuals who wouldn't normally have power over our lives to wreak serious havoc. Serious bullying experiences are often tied to a trauma response. Research I had done in my local community mental health agency demonstrated that an enormous portion of the children and youth that were brought to the mental health crisis center identified being bullied as the reason for their mental health crisis (often expressed in the form of suicidal or homicidal ideation). This reminded me at the time how incredibly important it is that we recognize the impact bullying can have on our emotional health and wellbeing.

Sexual Violence: Sexual violence often falls under the domain of child abuse or domestic partner violence. Other forms of sexual violence very well could fall under the heading of community violence. Sexual violence crosses all cultural and economic barriers.

Medical (illness or accident): Dealing with the negative impact of a health crisis (either a significant but short-term illness or a chronic condition) can be intensely traumatic. There's the loss of function and freedom from the health problem itself, and then there's the stress of accessing needed care and struggling to pay for it. Individuals with chronic, debilitating diseases which can be treated but not cured have to struggle with coming to terms with a "new normal," and many know that this disease will eventually no longer be treatable—and the decline accompanying that experience is terrifying.

Natural or Human-made Disasters: Natural disasters are events such as tornadoes, earthquakes, and floods that wreak havoc on our communities. Human-made disasters have a similar impact, but are the result of human action or inaction (such as industrial accidents like Chernobyl or the Exxon Valdez spill). There can be significant overlap between the two, as failure in planning for or engaging in appropriate action during or after a natural disaster worsens the consequences, leaking into being a man-made disaster (i.e., studies of the Hurricane Katrina floods demonstrate that the majority of the flooding was due to faulty levees installed by the US Army Corps of Engineers, not the hurricane itself).

War/Terrorism: The standard definitions of these terms assume that war is engaged in between willing participants with agreed-upon terms, while terrorism is conducted by renegades and targets innocent bystanders. Clearly, this isn't an accurate definition . . . however, the perception of one form of violence being more acceptable than the other has often led to a lack of understanding about the trauma inherent in both. While we expect and empathize with the suffering of the innocent bystander, the individuals who willingly serve as soldiers are also likely to struggle with PTSD or other trauma-related symptoms. According to the VA, 10-30% of soldiers have suffered PTSD sometime during their return home after being in a conflict (the statistics vary based on the service era). The US Department of Veterans Affairs released a statistic in 2013, citing approximately 22 veteran suicides occurring per day. No matter our role in such situations, the impact can be devastating.

Forced Displacement: We are sometimes forced to leave the only place we have known as home. Oftentimes these reasons are for our own safety, but it can still be traumatic. It is important to remember that whether you are leaving war-torn Syria as a refugee or being placed in a foster home due to a parent's inability to provide adequate care, leaving your home and community is a trauma in and of itself. No matter how dire the circumstances, being placed in new and unfamiliar surroundings and leaving the only home you have ever known requires a huge shift in thinking and behavior that is intensely difficult.

Traumatic Grief/Bereavement: While grief is a normal part of the human experience, some people's struggle with intense loss in a similar way to other traumatic events, and they are unable to process the loss in a way that allows them to move forward.

Systems Trauma: Individuals who are subject to some sort of system are also at risk for a trauma response. For example, children in foster care or the juvenile justice system may struggle with the trauma associated with the events that resulted in their entering the system, the trauma of the displacement experience, and then the continued trauma of having very little power and control over their experience within the system. Not knowing what your future will look like, being unable to form support networks due to continued movement and staff turnover, and not being able to obtain accurate information about your situation are all common experiences. A system itself often perpetuates its own, ongoing form of trauma that cannot be discounted when we look at the experiences that shape us.

Intergenerational Trauma: Historical oppression and its consequences are often transmitted down generations. This can happen through continued poverty and lack of opportunity in communities (such as Indian reservations), as well as within our literal genetic code. Trauma experienced by our parents and grandparents has the capacity to change our epigenetic structure in utero, causing many individuals to be born with a hardwired trauma response.

These are just some of the things that can be a trauma. In the end, we all experience trauma differently, and are impacted by too many things to list. Creating a list that touches only on the big "diagnosable" categories dismisses other experiences that shouldn't be dismissed.

So this list is intended to start conversations, and maybe help you realize the legitimacy of some life experiences as being traumatic. And while my list is more inclusive than one you will read in the DSM, it may not fit your circumstances. And trauma doesn't operate by checking the right box in the right category. So I hope that you will believe me when I say *your experiences and reactions are valid and real and you are worthy of care and the opportunity to heal.*

References

Brown, C., & Augusta-Scott, T. (2007). Narrative therapy: Making meaning, making lives. Thousand Oaks: SAGE.

Fanon, F., Philcox, R., Sartre, J., & Bhabha, H. K. (2017). The wretched of the earth. Cape Town: Kwela Books.

Gadotti, M., Gomez, M. V., & Freire, L. (2004). Lecciones de Paulo Freire: Cruzando fronteras: Experiencias que se completan. Buenos Aires: CLACSO.

Johnstone, L. & Boyle, M. with Cromby, J., Dillon, J., Harper, D., Kinderman, P., Longden, E., Pilgrim, D. & Read, J. (2018). The Power Threat Meaning Framework: Towards the identification of patterns in emotional distress, unusual experiences and troubled or troubling behaviour, as an alternative to functional psychiatric diagnosis. Leicester: British Psychological Society.

Jordan, J. V. (1991). The movement of mutuality and power. Wellesley, MA: Stone Center, Wellesley College.

Jordan, J. V., Hartling, L. M., & Walker, M. (2004). The complexity of connection: Writings from the Stone Centers Jean Baker Miller Training Institute. New York: Guilford Press.

Tyson, L. (2015). Critical theory today: A user-friendly guide. Milton Park, Abingdon, Oxon: Routledge.

Watkins, M., & Shulman, H. (2010). Toward psychologies of liberation. Basingstoke: Palgrave Macmillan.

MICROCOSM · PUBLISHING

Microcosm Publishing is Portland's most diversified publishing house and distributor with a focus on the colorful, authentic, and empowering. Our books and zines have put your power in your hands since 1996, equipping readers to make positive changes in their lives and in the world around them. Microcosm emphasizes skill-building, showing hidden histories, and fostering creativity through challenging conventional publishing wisdom with books and bookettes about DIY skills, food, bicycling, gender, self-care, and social justice. What was once a distro and record label was started by Joe Biel in his bedroom and has become among the oldest independent publishing houses in Portland, OR. We are a politically moderate, centrist publisher in a world that has inched to the right for the past 80 years.

What abilities do you have that you didn't have in the past?

What resources do you have that you didn't have in the past?

What power do you have that cannot be taken from you regardless of your circumstances?

How would you describe who and where you are at this moment in your life?